I Will Teach You To Become Rich:

Don't Get A Job Make A Job

Job

DAVE MCALLEN

Amazon Kindle Direct Publishing, USA.
Email: davemcallenz@yahoo.com
Copyright © 2020 by Dave McAllen

ISBN: 9798688141986

DEDICATION

To organizations and entities who tutored me to find the
path to wealth

CONTENTS

ACKNOWLEDGMENTS

The author wishes to thank all students of this course and readers   for investing in themselves. You won't be disappointed.

1. INTRODUCTION

Congratulations you made it here. I promised you a guaranteed job that will make you thousands or even millions and I will give you what I promised. Before we get deeper, I want to prepare your mind again fear of having plenty of money.

I want you to get the right outlook on matters. You will be making a lot of money. I don't want you to become afraid of making money. You will be charging people and giving them what they want. Don't let your conscience worry you because you charge people so much. You have what they need. You took out your time to make it available for them. So, they have to pay for it.

I really want that to sink into your head because it happened to me. When I began to see the kind of money that I've never seen before, I was afraid of money at first. "Dave, why are you charging people?" I was querying myself. But in time, I was able to get the right mindset and I wasn't bothered anymore. Yes, people pay for my products because they need them. It's not because they want to help me. I charge for them because I know that my clients care about my products and not about me. I charge very high. It's only on Amazon that I have low cost products because I have to compare mine with related products.

So, I don't want you to have this experience. I don't want so much money to shock you. You have the right to get money for your labour. You'll make so much money that you will never go to look for a job outside your own industry.

I will tell you exactly how you can earn thousands from creating a job for yourself. I will tell you the kind of job that is making me tens of thousands every month and how I did it. The best jobs you can create are digital products industry and online services.

I am doing both. So I can assure you that you will make thousands from it. As a beginner, you won't earn less than a thousand dollars in a month if you follow what I will show you. None of my students of this course or who read this guide earns less than that at the beginning. You can be sure that you won't earn less than that if you follow everything that I am going to show you.

You won't have problems placing your jobs too. I will show you where to showcase it and how to generate traffic of the right people to patronize you.

As I said before, I recommend Two wealth making

Jobs

1. Digital product industry and
2. Online services.

Let's   learn   what   this   is   about.

2. MAKE THE JOB

This is not going to be as difficult as you may think. You don't need some special skills to be able to create a money making job. Just pay attention to everything I'm going to show you. I will also show you where you can get others to do the work for you if you don't know what to do. That's Fiverr.

In the next topic I am going to start with the first money making job you can set up for yourself. That is the digital products industry.

3. DIGITAL PRODUCTS INDUSTRY

This is one job that is paying very high and it's not very competitive. I will explain what I mean when I said "not very competitive". When you set up this industry, you will be able to create two highly sought-for products: (1) Digital Books blueprint and (2) Video guide and video courses.

This has very low competition if you pay attention and enter the industry from the point I'm going to show you. We all know that there are billions of books and videos in the market today. But what your industry is going to be creating are not just books and videos like every other ones. People are going to be looking for your own. You are going to take your time to be searching out people's wounds. And you are going to be searching for the healing for those wounds. And when you find them, you are going to be offering them in your products. So, instead of looking for customers for your products, they will go looking for you because of your special products.

You can see why I said that your niche is going to have very low competition. But how are you going to locate people's pains? And how are you going to find the cure for the pains? Calm down I will show you how to do this with ease. First, I will show you the craziest moneymaking niches to target with your books and videos. They are only four. You will get your materials for any topic from Google and YouTube. So, you won't need to crack your head for what to write about. Then, I will also teach you how to generate more traffic to your showstore. So, you are going to be creating special products, unlike what is common out there. And customers will look for them. And you will be making your thousands.

The four hottest niches to target are

1. Health
2. Travel
3. Relationship
4. Online marketing

As I said before, your digital products industry is going to be creating Digital Books Blueprint, Video Guides and Video Courses. I will be talking about digital book blueprint first, in the next topic. Let's meet there.

4. DIGITAL BOOK BLUEPRINT

Before creating your digital book, you must be sure that it's going to sell very well. We have a way of confirming that your book will sell once it hit the market. You have to first of all ascertain people's pains in the niche. How do we do this?

The Pre-creation Process

People often say they are looking for a profitable niche to target or profitable keywords to target. That's wrong. We don't look for niches or keywords to target. Rather, we look for people's frustrations and when we find them, we target them with our products, in this case, our books. People's pains, frustrations and woes are our keywords. Let me give you an example.

Relationship is a high paying keyword. But it's a wide subject. So, you need to narrow it down. Use Google trends with keywords pro and publishers rocket to investigate. Start with the broad subject like

RELATIONSHIP. Then, scroll through the results. You will find some search results that won't really sell your products. You might see something like "how to make the girl look at you", "how to tell a guy 'no'", etc. Those questions might have been queried just to satisfy curiosity.

But when you see something like "how can I make the guy marry me?" or "how can I save my marriage", these suggest that the persons involved are in trouble. This is how to investigate people's frustrations and target them. The research tools will also show you how many times people search for those terms in a month. The higher the searches, the better for your products. Later, I will show you how to do this properly and other things to look for before you target a wound.

But so far, you have seen that you don't start creating a digital product just because you think that it's something people will like. If you do that you may end up being the only reader of your book. So, we don't encourage that. You don't need to like the subject. But that is what will bring you money.

Let's start with getting the title of your digital book blueprint.

Generating Product Title

The title of your digital book product is also very important. One of your keywords can be your main title and another, your subtitle. But your title has to be power words. They should be attention grabbing words. Your title should be able to mention the frustration and then promise a positive result.

Before creating one of my latest books on Amazon, I researched into stress. I found a trend where increased number of people are trying to avoid frequent use of medicine for stress. So, I went ahead and titled the book, "Relieve Stress Without Medicine". What about this book in your hand? People want a certain lifestyle for themselves and they need a good income flow to support it. So, I appropriately call this, "I Will Teach You To Become Rich". Attention grabbing indeed!

Your title need power words. See some examples and ask yourself which of the set of words is more powerful:

Consider Vs Get

Employment Vs Job

Think Vs Dream

Expired Vs Dead

New Vs Untapped

Mate Vs Sex

Build up Vs Create

The point is that power words helps to grab the attention of anyone who sees the title of your digital book product. Use the keyword research tools that I mentioned – google trends, keywords research pro, publishers rocket. Some of them are paid research tools, but they are also more than 1000% money back. Later, I will show you where to use each of the keyword tools. It's going to depend on where you place your digital products.

Creating Your Book Content

As I already taught you, your goal is to give people quality products, exactly what you promised. You have to locate the pains and frustrations of people. Then, you must work hard to find the solution for them, by spending time on research. That way, you solve their problem as you promised and get paid for it.

Later, I will teach you the difference between using Amazon or your personal website to showcase your digital products. I mentioned it now because where you take your customers to buy your products determines the tools you are going to use for your keywords which in turn dictates the materials for the contents of your digital book product.

If you will be taking your customers to Amazon, you will use publishers rocket as your research tool. But if you will be sending them to your own website, you will have to use the other two, google trends and keywords research pro.

Once you Search out the pain points of the people with the appropriate tools, you can use some of these keywords as the chapter titles for your book content.

Our main reservoir of content for any topic is YouTube and google articles. Take each keyword of your chapter title and search it in YouTube. Look at several videos until you get the one that is right for that chapter topic. Make sure it also contributes to the overall objectives of the entire product. Do the same for the other chapter titles until you are done with all of them.

You can also search for blog articles on google that you can use. Modify them to suit the objective of your product.

Pay attention to this point. You need an introduction that welcomes and congratulates your reader. Tell them that they made a good choice buying the product. If you like mention the name of your product. Then emphasize your promise again to give them what you promised. At the end of every chapter summarize what they learned in one or two sentences and create anticipation for what they will learn in the next. And use the first paragraph from chapter two onward, and create a one or two sentence summary of the preceding chapter and a short introduction of the current chapter. This helps readers to retain what they learn and relate them to one another in logical order.

Finally, create your conclusion. This should thank the readers for staying with you in the journey. Then, it should state what was learned in the course and the value of the information. And a few lines should motivate the reader to take action based on what he learned so that he can get the results that you promised. If you want them to contact you after, leave your email. Email is better. I don't want you to give anyone access to your private number. I learned my lesson about that.

At the start, I didn't know that people will read my

books. So I gave out all my contacts in a bid to getting people to speak with me about my books. I felt that would be great if people can really call and tell me something about my book. Soon, I lost my privacy and peace. People can even call at the middle of the night. I don't want you to suffer that. If you follow my guide and create quality products, people will keep coming for them and many would like to speak with you. Give them your email and not your number. You need time to keep creating new products and not one to answer calls.

How long will it take you to create a product content? In one day, you can create your book content. I get mine ready in one day. But as a beginner if you complete yours in two or three days, it's okay. For a product that will earn you thousands, two or three days is okay.

If you don't know how to write, you can get someone to do it for you on Fiverr.com. All you need to do is the keyword research. Then, someone on Fiverr will organize it into a quality book content for you and you pay him. You put your name on it, and it becomes your book.

I always emphasize quality content. Exactly what you promised. This way, the money you are making won't bother your mind.

The next thing I want to talk about is the cover for you digital book product.

Creating a Clean Cover

Good covers also sell products. Like your book

content, your placement determines how your cover will look like. For books on Amazon, you will need a 2D type of cover. But if you will be selling your digital book product on your own website, the best cover type is a mockup, which is 3D.

Amazon cover formatting guideline will give you options of what you want, either to Do It Yourself or to use the KDP cover creator. I usually recommend doing it yourself. This gives you the liberty to create your cover the way you want it to be. If you use the KDP cover creator, you will be limited in what you can do.

To get the best cover for your digital book product, use this secret I want to show you. You already know your niche and the keywords that relate to that niche. From your Publishers Rocket, select two or three Book that are ranking high on the niche that relates to your book. Try as much as possible to mimic the cover of that one when creating your own cover. Look at the cover image, the background and the cover text fonts. That way, you have already diverted some of the buyers of that book to buy your own book product.

Tools For Your Amazon Book Cover

I use a mobile cover design tool. The one I use is called PIXELAB. It is very simple to use and it has everything you want to create a clean cover.

I get the images I use from a website called pixabay.com. There, you can get free images to use for commercial purposes without any attribution.

Each time you download an image, they will ask you for a cup of coffee. It's voluntary. If you have, you give, and if you don't have, no problem. All contributors are asked to sign an agreement with Creative Common Laws, which allows other people to use any image they submitted for free. So you won't have any copyright infringement issues if you use their free images. T

Pixabay also has paid images from Shutterstock, if you want to pay for images. But I use free ones. All their images are quality images, both free and paid. But as I said, I use free ones. You can decide what you want.

For Kindle eBooks, the cover dimensions is usually 1600 X 2560 pixel. But if you need to have a print book for additional income, there are different dimensions. You have 5 X 8, 6 X 9, etc. They also have templates to format your cover, if you want to do it yourself. But if you are using KDP cover creator for your print book, that is allowed and it's simple. After choosing the trim size for your interior, you launch the cover creator next and select use image from your computer. That will take you to your computer where you can select the image you already created for your eBook. You will follow the rest of the process and the cover creator will apply the eBook cover for your print book front cover.

Next, complete the review process and publish your book.

But if you have the skills to use CorelDraw or Adobe Photoshop, good! But if you don't have, PIXELAB doesn't require any special skills to use. You get the same high quality cover and effects that you need. PIXELAB can be downloaded from Google Playstore.

Tools for Creating a Mockup Cover

Mockup covers are the best if you will be selling your digital book product on your website. They are 3D in shape. They give readers a sense of reading a book even though they know that it's a digital book. We are humans and that's the way we feel.

So, mockup generators are very common. You can get them for free for both PC and mobile. You know how to get that so I don't want to waste time on that. They are also easy to use once you download and install them. What you have to do is create a 2D cover first, like the one I taught you to create for Kindle eBook. Something like this. This is a portrait. The white background is not letting it show full. But you know what a portrait should look like. I have many pen names. It's Dan Williams I used in this product.

GET SICKLE CELL
REMEDY
WITHOUT
MARROW
TRANSPLANT

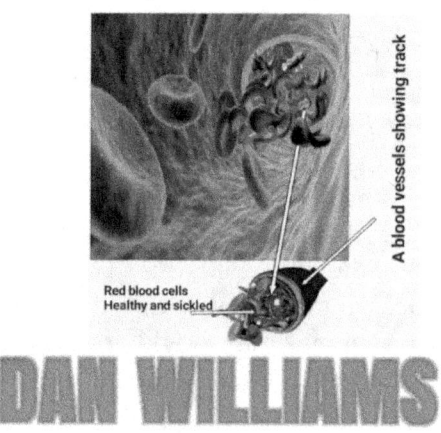

A blood vessels showing track

Red blood cells
Healthy and sickled

DAN WILLIAMS

Next, upload it to your mockup generator and select the thickness you want. That will make the front cover into something like a print book image. Something like this below.

You can then create another one to be showing the cover on a tablet or an eReader such as the one you see here.

You can add shadow to show like a book standing in a lit room. Then, incline the eReader cover against the book and use them together as your book cover on your website. I want you to do something like this.

This is the type of cover that's good for digital book products on your website. Place it on the book page on your website. Insert it also at the beginning of your book interior content in Microsoft Word before printing it to PDF. Your digital book product to sell on your website should usually be in PDF format. All devices will be able to read it in PDF.

Overall, covers must be clean just like the examples I just showed you. And make sure that all your writings on the covers are visible and readable.

This is how you create a book product for your digital industry. These books make me hundreds everyday. And they will make the same for you if you follow everything I'm teaching you. For the first one or two months, you're going to be getting nothing less than a thousand. But as you continue, you will find that your goal will be higher. And you can meet them, depending on the kind of lifestyle you want. My goal is 50k every month. I made it and crossed it at the heart of lockdown. I'm working hard to stabilize it right now.

Before we talk about your showstore where you will be sending your customers, let me show you how to create the second type of products in your digital industry. That's the video guides and video courses. This is another product that's making me much money.

5. VIDEO GUIDES AND VIDEO COURSES

Why will people buy your videos when they are available for free on YouTube? I had the same thought when I learned that video guides and video courses make good money. Then, I learned the untapped secret. And that is what I'm showing you now.

Even though there are free videos and free information on the web, they are scattered. A person who is not writing a book or making a video will not be interested in taking the time to gather them together just to use one-off. We found that more than 95% of the people who look for information are not interested in scattered thoughts and ideas. They prefer to pay some money and have the information where it's gathered together in one place. The money to pay is not their problem. Their wounds that decays every moment is their care. Their pains and their frustrations are their concern. If they find promise for the positive results they want, they will readily part with some money no matter what you call it. You can testify to this. If you wanted to go looking for scattered information, you won't buy this book you are reading right now.

So, when your digital industry make a video guide or video course, there are people who are looking for these videos already. That is why video products are making a hell of money. Later on, I will show you where to sell your videos. YouTube is out of it. Keep this in mind. Instagram is also out of it. People are just there to watch and like videos and pictures. You will place your videos in places where value can be place on it.

It's similar to creating your digital book product for your industry. You must first search and search to locate people's deep frustrations. Don't gather materials for pleasure seeking people. Build your materials around people who have pains, severe ones. As I said before, the most profitable niches are:

HEALTH

TRAVEL

ONLINE MARKETING

RELATIONSHIP

Get narrower with your keywords search. Does the search terms say:

Shrink prostate naturally without surgery? The pain is the fear of being operated on. Get a visa to Canada under $350? These people's frustration is poverty. They may be persons in developing countries who wish to go abroad in search of greener pastures. Which online business can make me good cash? The woes of these set may be debt, jobs or low income. There are also queries that show pain in a relationship. These are what your industry should target with videos. And video courses should be able to focus on practical skills that people are crazy about.

Increasing number of people are taking courses through videos. So, if your industry creates a video product on courses, you are sure to make a lot of money. You don't need to be an expert in these courses. No. I have already shown you how you can gather quality materials to build a pile of valuable information. This is what you teach in your videos. If you can't gather quality materials, pay a little on Fiverr for others to do it for you after your keywords and title research.

The second type of videos that are high paying are guides. People need information about a lot of issues. Like I said before, it is difficult for them to find the information in one place. When you search for these information and gather them to one place, these people who are looking for it will willingly pay to have it.

So, you won't need to be an expert or to crack your brain for what to show on your industry video product. You don't need to be the source of the ideas. But you research them and build a new and logical ideas set. So, the new result is yours. Put your name on it and begin to sell it as long as you didn't copy the work of another person. You learned the ideas and modified it to suit the objectives of your products.

Next Step

Show your face on the camera Teach these ideas in your guides and courses in the eyes of a camera. When the lectures are ready, begin to distribute them. And you will start to make a lot of money from them.

Tools for Creating Your Video Products

I don't recommend using YouTube for creating your industry videos. YouTube has low video quality. And your videos will be visible for everyone to see. So, no one will be willing to pay money for it on your website. Another shortfall of YouTube video is it's distraction. If you place it on your site, when visitors click on it, they are taken away from you site. They won't be redirected back to your site.

The tool I usually recommend is Vimeo. It has free and paid account. You can upgrade whenever you want. Their videos are of very high quality. And you can hide your videos from the public. In that way, only a person who pays for it can have access to it.

In the next topic, we are going talk about where you display your products. This is where your industry will direct customers. Before then, I want us to look at other things to consider when choosing keywords.

6. KEYWORDS RESEARCH

Don't ever try to use your head to choose keyword ideas. I have shown you the keywords tools that I use to sell my products. Google trends, keywords research pro and publishers rocket. These are valuable too. I also use Ahrefs.

If a keyword contains the text that you would like to target, you need to check for other elements. All the keyword research tools will show you how many times people search for those terms in one month. Google Trends will show you the pattern of search over a period according to how you set the filter. Publishers Rocket and Ahrefs will show you KD, that's the keyword difficulty. Publishers Rocket will show you how many books are ranking for a keyword.

With all this ideas in mind, you can see that there are keywords you can target and your products will never show up to anyone. That's why, it's important to use a keyword tool rather than using your head.

If the search per month is high, it means that people are searching for a product on that search term very well. Ahrefs can show you the KD. It is usually on a scale of 0 to 100. The higher the KD, the higher the competition for that keyword and the more difficult it will be for your product to rank well and sell on that keyword. Choose a keyword with high monthly searches and a low KD. Publishers Rocket shows the KD, the monthly searches, the number of books that are ranking for the keyword, as well as the average monthly earnings of the keyword.

If you are searching for keyword for a book, you now know what to do after getting this information. A keyword with high average monthly searches, low difficulty few products on in and high monthly average earnings is the best. This will make your book show up on the first page and begin to sell in high numbers everyday.

If your product is created to sell on Amazon, there's one final thing to do. The average monthly searches that you have on Publishers Rocket is based on a 12 month period. But people no longer search for some keywords maybe after 3, 4 months. That's why keywords are tweaked and updated regularly.

So, before using your selected keywords on Amazon, make sure you conduct one last keyword test to see if customers are currently searching for it or it has expired.

Open your browser. Go to incognito mode. Enter

amazon.com. set the search bar to kindle store. Start typing a keyword. If the keyword is included in the search suggestions before you finished typing, use the keyword. It means people are currently searching for it. But if it doesn't, don't use it. The keyword has expired.

Set the bar again to book. Conduct the same test for your printbook keywords. Use the active ones and discard the dead ones. Now you're all set to have a good sale.

Just follow what I'm showing you. You will win. Your industry will make a lot of cash for you. That's what is making me thousands every month.

Let's now look at where you will be sending your customers to buy your products.

7. YOUR DIGITAL INDUSTRY SHOWSTORE

A virtual industry is similar to a real one. Like a real industry, your digital products need a placement or showroom. This is where you send your customers to buy them. I use four of them and I will also want you to use them.

1. Amazon KDP. If you use Amazon as your landing store, you won't have to do anything other than simply creating your book products and publishing them.
2. Your own website. You will need to create one. But it's easy. I will show some cheap web host.
3. Affiliate websites. You won't need to do anything after creating your products. Others will sell for you and you will earn 50 to 60 percent of the sales.
4. Udemy.

If your digital industry creates books, they can be sold on Amazon, your own website and on Affiliate websites. Your video guide and video courses can be sold on your website and on Udemy.

8. GETTING PRODUCT ONTO THE SHOWSTORE

On Amazon KDP you have little to do as I said before. Create an author or publishers account. Get started. By now I believe you must have created a book product. On your dashboard, you will see where to start to create an eBook on the left section of the page. If you click on it, you will be guided through the process of creating your eBook and publishing it on KDP.

Please, one more area to pay attention to is the description of your book. It should not be too long. Create anticipation for what your book is offering. However, don't give out essential details. Leave your prospective buyer in suspense. Also insert keywords as many as you can control in a sentence into your description. Amazon algorithm will pick them up and rank your book for them. With all this done, your book will have chances for good visibility.

Your Own Website create your own website. I will give you a host that takes as low as $4 per month https://www.interserver.net/ purchase a domain and hosting. You might spend as low as $17 for getting the website.

Once you do that, install WordPress and chose a simple theme for your page. There are many free themes you can choose from. I recommend total. Go to your admin dashboard. Highlight on appearance and click on customize. Click on theme and select total. That theme will be installed on your website. The other things are simple to do. So, don't let's waste much time here. What I particularly want to stress is the important plugins that you will need to install so that you can sell on your website. You will need:

A landing page import

Woocomerce

Automatewoo

Payment gateway

If you have these installed in your website you will be able to put products on your website and collect money directly into your account.

Just get a domain for your digital industry. Once you've done that, look at those things I mentioned to set up your website. Find time, play around with them. You will find that it's simple to set up your website to host or showcase your industry digital products. You especially need a website if your digital industry will be creating video guide and video courses.

Once you are done setting up your website, place your digital products on the landing pages. Link the price of each product from the product page to the checkout page. When people buy your product, the money goes to your account.

This is unlike selling on Amazon or on an affiliate website where you share your earnings with others. If you sell on your website, you are going to have the whole money to yourself. On your own website too, you can charge very high. That's the secret. That makes people value your product.

This is what you have to do if you want to sell on your website.

Selling Through Affiliate Websites. In this too, your industry doesn't have much to do more than creating quality products and offering them to affiliate marketers. There are several affiliate websites. But I will give you the one I used. They are very good. They have created a ready marketing network. So, when your books come, they melt naturally into the system. You can decide to share the earnings at 60:40 or 50:50 ratio. With fifty fifty, you get more aggressive marketers for your products. And you are paid every Friday. expertnaire.com. But your industry can't sell videos on affiliate websites.

Udemy. This is one of the most crowded video websites. You find people looking to buy video guides or video courses. And it's also a platform for those who have the ones to sell. You sell yours there and make your money.

As I told you before, you don't need to be an expert to sell videos lectures on Udemy. I have taught you how to get ideas for your videos. If you have rich information to lecture on your videos, people are looking for it. Create the video and touch people's lives with it. Put a good price on your video products – $29.99, $39.99, $49.99. You can even sell some videos at $99.99. Later, I will tell you the rational behind this price pattern.

Don't be afraid to give high prices for your products. If it touches people's wounds and then promise to heal them, they will pay any amount to get the results. So, don't be afraid of calling money for your products. You will earn hundreds, even thousands daily. Checkout the price I placed on this product on my website. GET REMEDY FOR SICKLE CELL WITHOUT MARROW TRANSPLANT is $17.99. It's a PDF eBook. Oh wao! That price seems high. But guess what? People are buying it like mad. Nobody has ever thought of sickle cell as having any remedy. So, my book is a special product.

Yes, I did my research very well and I was able to unlock a therapy that doesn't just manage but reverses sickle cell and related problems. I quickly bagged into it. I would have even made it 59.79 or higher but I found that many Sicklers are poor.

So, that's what I mean. When you look for a deep pain and find a solution to it, blow it open and begin to call money for it.

These are your Showstores. In the next topic, we will be talking about leading the right people to your products.

9. SENDING TRAFFIC TO YOUR SHOWSTORE

Our major source of traffic is facebook advertisement. But you don't need this for your Amazon Showstore or Udemy or Affiliate websites. Your keywords and tags will give you high organic sales if you have followed the secrets that I showed you. But if you have set up your website, you will need it and you will make at least four times your ads spent, daily. Trust me. It's what I do. I don't want to share any now because I use a lot of pen names. I don't want to give myself away. But I will show you how to run these ads on Facebook and make your money.

Okay, I need to show you one. You can explore this product that I created last month. GET SICKLE CELL REMEDY WITHOUT MARROW TRANSPLANT. valueztapper.com. The pen names I used on that product is Dan Williams. As I said, I have many of them and they are all making money for me. That too is one of my websites. I just revealed that one to you for the purpose of this course. But, I don't like to share them. Those looking for them, will get them. I don't want anyone to link them to one person because I am making a lot from them. If you work hard like this too, you will be afraid to let people know that you are making so much money. And if they know your pennames and all you're your sites, they will be able to measure your wealth. I created that product I just mentioned last month. Guess what! It has earned me almost seventeen. That's less than one month.

Don't wonder why ads is good. Coca-Cola is still running ads till tomorrow. If you have a good product and wait for the customers to come, that's a bad way of marketing. But a proactive marketer don't wait for the customers to come. He creates a good product and puts it in front of the customers. That's an old trick that big industries still use till date. They spend a lot of money running ads. They're not fools. I'll teach you how to run Facebook ads profitably and earn more than four times your ads spent.

In front Of The Right Customers

You need to set your product in front of the customers. Facebook ads for your personal website Showstore is one medium to do that. Amazon Countdown deal and Amazon Campaign is the one for Amazon Showstore. Twitter, facebook and Instagram for Udemy Showstore. But for affiliate marketing, they will do the job for you.

How To Target The Right People With

Facebook Ads

You need a Facebook page. A Facebook page is different from Facebook personal profile. A page is for business, and so, you can run ads on it. But you can't run an ad on personal profile. You will also need to create and add account ad a Facebook pixel. After creating a page, go to the homepage of your Facebook account. Scroll down to Ads Manager. Click on it. A dashboard will open. Because you have no previous ads, no running ads or completed one will show on your dashboard. So you will have to create one.

Facebook Ads Creating Process

By now, you must have added a credit or debit card to your ads account. It's from the card you'll be charged for your ads.

As I said before, go to your Facebook account homepage. Scroll down to Ads manager. Click on it to go to your ads dashboard. You will find no previous ads. Click on create ads.

When the ads placement page opens, they will ask for the objective of your ads. Select conversation. This way, Facebook will not be sending visitors to like your page or chat with you or comment on your post. They will be sending your visitors to click and go to your website to buy your products.

After selecting conversation, turn off automatic targeting. Otherwise, Facebook will be sending your ads to any person on the site who might not be interested in your product.

Next select manual targeting. That will allow you to choose who you want Facebook to show your ads to.

For budget, choose between 5 and 10 dollars a day. Don't be afraid. You will earn at least, 4 times more than that, trust me. I earn 10 to 15 times with some products. So, you can't earn less than 4 times your ads spent for a start. But the higher your budget the more your visitors and the more you earn.

Give a name to your ad. This will help you to identify it buy the time you create several of them.

For placement uncheck everything except. Mobile and news feed. Don't allow Facebook to show your ads on desktop, on Instagram, in website news, etc. Choose only mobile and news feed. Otherwise, Facebook will be showing your ads to where people will not see it and your money will be burning for nothing.

When they ask for your pixel, select your pixel. Something to note about Facebook pixel. After creating your pixel, make sure you copy your pixel ID and place it on your website. That will help you to track how your Facebook ads are performing. Pixel links your Facebook ads to your website.

For location, choose the country of the people who may be interested in your products. Be specific. That is why you turned off automatic targeting. You know who will be interested in your products. Facebook doesn't. They would show your ads to just anyone if you leave automatic targeting on and they will take their money.

As I said, be specific. For location, you can choose United States, for example. But don't stop there. Facebook will like to show your ads to those living in the selected country and those recently in the country. Don't accept that. Select only those living in the country. Strangers or visitors won't be interested in products created for people living in a country. Ads shown to them would most likely be a waste.

When asked for gender, select "All" (that's men and women) except if your product is for a particular gender.

The age group you want to sell you product to also matters. They should be persons who can pay for something. So, chose between 20 and 55 years. These age bracket has what it takes to buy and understands digital operations.

Next, choose dynamic ads. This is better. Dynamic ads type allows you to creates several ads at the same time, varying their pictures and text. When you publish, Facebook will be testing the ads sets one after the other. It will finally stick to the one that has the best results. That helps you to maximize profit.

So, you need to give name to your ad set apart from the ad's name. This arises when you are about to choose your audience. The name should relate to the kind of audience that you want for that ad set. For example, if you want to target with your ads, people who want to burn fat, you can call that ad set, obese persons.

The next thing you are going to do is to narrow your

audience to include only the people that are relevant to your product. Now, search for audience that are related to the ad set. When you start to type something in the audience search bar, Facebook will suggest relevant searches in recent time. Select the ones that apply. You will immediately see your potential audience on the left side of the page.

Continue to add audience until you reach a sizeable potential audience. A carefully selected audience that's between 2 million and 10 million is best. Below this potential audience, you will see your potential daily reach and potential daily sale. If you increase your budget, these daily values will increase.

On the final page, add the image of your product. Add the text of your ad.

The text of the ad should be carefully crafted. The ad title should be attention grabbing. And the first sentence should mention a frustration point and promise to offer a solution. For example, you can mention: SHRINK PROSTATE WITH UNDER $200 TREATMENT. Prostate is the frustration and $200 is a low-cost solution. Next, list 3 or 4 negatives that will be eliminated and 3 or 4 positive results your product has. Say that the offer if for a limited time. Make wise use of emojis. (⬜⬜⬜⬜⬜⬜✔⬜ ⬜⬜⬜) to add feeling to your add text.

When you are asked about where you want to send you audience, fill in your website URL (yourwebsite.com)

Preview your ad and then publish.

When your ad has run for a while, you can go back to check the gender that's buying your products most. You can also see in which state of the country, the age group and what Facebook takes to sell a product in a particular location. Take a log of this and create another ad. Target the age groups, the state and the age that profits you most. This way, you properly utilize your ad spent and maximize sales.

I hope this is going to help your digital industry sell her book, video guides and video courses and make hundreds or even thousands for you daily. That's what it makes for me and others who follow this guide.

Amazon Ads

Amazon offers you opportunities to get exposure for your book products. If you want to get access to free promotion or countdown deal, your book products must be enrolled on KDP SELECT. You can enroll while creating your kindle book or after your book is published. Each term runs for 90 days during which period you can give your book products for free for any five days you want. You can also choose to automatically continue your enrollment or stop after 90 days by checking or unchecking the box at the KDP SELECT manager.

Amazon also offers you the chance to offer your book at discount prices over a period of several days. This is available for a limited Amazon marketplaces. This promotion is also very easy to create.

KDP also allows you to run paid ads for your book

products. For this, you will need to create an ads account and add a credit or debit card from which your ads will be charged.

The beauty of Amazon ads is that you will never be charged unless your ads is click buy a potential buyer.

As I said before, it's your choice. You don't need a paid ads or to give your book products for free in order to sell. With the keyword research tools that I have shown you, you will get organic sales even without ads. However, many big-time Amazon sellers also use ads to generate millions of dollars. So, if you want, you can learn it an run paid ads for your digital products on Amazon Showstore.

I want to assure you, this is a million dollars making job you have just created for yourself.

Sending Traffic To Udemy Showstore

Remember that you have two places to sell your video guides and video courses. They are your website and Udemy. If you sell on your website Facebook ads is the main source to get people to buy your videos and it doesn't fail. But if you have the videos on Udemy, you don't need a paid ad. You can share your video links on Twitter, or Facebook or on Instagram. You can also spread the it with word of mouth or anywhere you normally have presence whether physical or virtual. And your videos will sell like crazy.

10. PRICE TRICKS AND DISCOUNT MAGIC

After showing you how to set your price, I said that I will explain to you the reason behind the price pattern. If you intend to sell a product at $10, set it to $9.99. It's the same thing. But that means a lot to your customers. It creates that feeling that there's discount on the product. They know that it's the same thing. But that won't reflect in their action. Their mind will keep telling them that there's discount.

So, if you have determined the price of your product, if does well for you taking a point off it. You will be touching the human psychology and stirring feelings to   produce   intended   effect.

COURSE SUMMARY

Over a few pages now, we have been together on a trip. What we just completed is how you can create a digital product industry for yourself and start earning thousands. It's what makes me thousands every month. And it will make it for you too. But you need to take action. By now, you should have created a product already.

You learned the two types of products your digital industry can create. They are digital book blueprint and videos (guides and courses). I have shown you how to create each product. They must be high quality products. They must be answers to people's pains and frustrations. They must heal deep wounds. If you work hard to get this information together in one place, you will be refreshed when they turn in thousands for you every month.

I also talked about the Showstores for your industry's products. They are: (1) your website which you can get cheap from the host that I showed you, interserver.net (2) KDP on Amazon, (3) Affiliate Websites and (4) Udemy.

You also learned how to drive the right people to your Showstore. They are Facebook, Amazon campaign programs and social media for Udemy products.

This earns a lot of money for me and my students. If you follow the secrets that I have shown you, you are going to be earning thousands too every month.

Some products can give you millions a month, depending on the wound you uncover and promised to heal.

I have done my part here. I'm supposed to sell this course higher than this. But I just gave it to you at a token. Why I did this is to help all of us to grow. I gave you everything. I spent a lot of money to learn some of these secrets some of which I added to this course for free. So, you need to take action so that all the effort doesn't become a waste.

Start by creating one product. You will start earning money immediately. Then proceed to creating another after the first. And on and on.

When you start making a lot of money, you can then decide the kind of life you want to live. You will be richer than estate agents. You don't need a capital like them. All the money you get is yours and doesn't offset any capital.

Buy the car of your dream, live in an area that you like. Take time off every month or quarterly or as you choose and tour the world. Just live as you desire.

So, what are you waiting? Start your digital products industry now. You will be at the top. And we will meet there, because that is where I'm going to be.

In the second book I will be talking about the second job of your dream. That is going to be

Online Services.

If you wish to contact me, send your message to:

davemcallenz@yahoo.com

Thanks for taking the course. Kindly rate and review my book. Thanks once again.

See you at the top.